GW00891013

WHSmith

National Test Practice Papers

Science

Graham Peacock

Age 10–11
Year 6
Key Stage 2

Contents	Page	Contents	Page

Hachette UK's policy is to use papers that are natural, renewable and recyclable products and made from wood grown in sustainable forests. The logging and manufacturing processes are expected to conform to the environmental regulations of the country of origin.

Orders: please contact Bookpoint Ltd, 130 Milton Park, Abingdon, Oxon OX14 4SB. Telephone: (44) 01235 827720. Fax: (44) 01235 400454. Lines are open 9.00a.m.–5.00p.m., Monday to Saturday, with a 24-hour message answering service. Visit our website at www.hoddereducation.co.uk.

© Graham Peacock 2013
First published in 2008 exclusively for WHSmith by
Hodder Education
An Hachette UK Company
338 Euston Road
London NW1 3BH

This second edition first published in 2013 exclusively for WHSmith by Hodder Education.

Impression number   10 9 8 7 6 5 4 3 2
Year   2018 2017 2016 2015 2014 2013

All rights reserved. Apart from any use permitted under UK copyright law, no part of this publication may be reproduced or transmitted in any form or by any means, electronic or mechanical, including photocopying and recording, or held within any information storage and retrieval system, without permission in writing from the publisher or under licence from the Copyright Licensing Agency Limited. Further details of such licences (for reprographic reproduction) may be obtained from the Copyright Licensing Agency Limited, Saffron House, 6–10 Kirby Street, London EC1N 8TS.

Cover illustration by Oxford Designers and Illustrators Ltd
Typeset by DC Graphic Design Ltd, Swanley Village, Kent
Printed in Great Britain by Hobbs the Printers Ltd, Totton, Hampshire SO40 3WX

A catalogue record for this title is available from the British Library.

ISBN: 978 1444 189 216

NOTE: The tests, questions and advice in this book are not reproductions of the official test materials sent to schools. The official testing process is supported by guidance and training for teachers in setting and marking tests and interpreting the results. The results achieved in the tests in this book may not be the same as are achieved in the official tests.

Science at Key Stage 2

There are five tests in this book, all of which are aimed at children performing at Levels 3 to 5. The first four tests give children who are likely to achieve Level 3 the chance to answer a range of questions. The last test is suitable only for very highly achieving pupils. Performance at the different levels is summarised below.

Level 3	Level 4	Level 5
Children can describe differences and provide simple explanations. They can sort materials and living things and offer ideas about why materials are suitable for their purpose. When explaining how things work they link cause and effect, such as suggesting that the lack of light causes plants to become yellow. They also make generalisations about things they see, such as suggesting that it is difficult to see dim lights if they are near very bright lights.	Children can use more scientific terms such as the names of the organs of the body and those of flowering plants. They can use technical terms to describe processes such as evaporation and condensation. They can explain how differences are used to classify materials and living things systematically. They use their ideas about the way the physical world works when explaining how shadows are formed or the way that sound is heard through different materials.	Children can explain the factors behind why different organisms are found in different environments. They can describe the properties of metals and how they are distinct from other materials. They can identify why changes occur in materials and can suggest ways in which specific mixtures can be separated. They can use abstract ideas and models to explain physical phenomena such as the orbiting model of the Earth to explain day and year length.

Setting the tests

Give your child plenty of time to do each test – 35 minutes should be about right.

These tests can be a chance to confirm how well your child has done and how much he or she has learnt. Don't focus exclusively on what the child does not know.

There are between 46 and 52 marks for each test. Enter the mark in the circle next to each question. Add the marks together at the end of each test and use them to assess your child's National Curriculum Level on pages 45 and 46.

Reviewing progress

Perhaps the best use of these tests is for your child to do one every month or two from September onwards during Year 6. Discuss the tests and the answers at the back of the book. Talk about how the science relates to everyday life. During the year, your child should make some progress. It is this improvement rather than the absolute marks or your child's marks compared with other children that you should concentrate on. However, be aware that achievement may vary as the context of each test is different.

Plants and animals

1 **a** Tick the living things in this list.

oak tree ☐   wheat ☐

salt ☐   crystal ☐

bee ☐   doll ☐

grass ☐   crocodile ☐

stone ☐

5

b Tick the plants in this list.

frog ☐   tulip ☐

pine tree ☐   blackbird ☐

beetle ☐   nettle ☐

carrot ☐   snail ☐

seaweed ☐   cactus ☐

6

c What are plants doing when they photosynthesise?

Tick one box.

They are making food from sunlight. ☐

They are making water from their roots. ☐

They are growing their leaves and flowers. ☐

1

TOTAL

◯

12

Bread and yeast

2 Class 5 make bread with a mixture of flour and water.

In one bowl they add yeast to the mixture.

In another bowl they do not add yeast.

Only the mixture with yeast rises.

a The children talk about the yeast.

They wonder if it was living.

Who is right?

Tick one box.

Jim	Yeast is alive because it feeds on flour.	☐
Kate	Yeast is a chemical which makes the bread rise.	☐
Paul	Yeast is not alive because it does not move and does not feed.	☐

1

Rotting

3 Some children keep two pieces of bread for a week:

- one piece is in a bag in a fridge
- one piece is in a bag in a warm place.

The one that was warm is covered in mould. The one from the fridge is fresh.

a Tick two correct ideas.

Mould likes to grow in the dark.	☐
Mould grows best in a warm place.	☐
Mould needs to be in a bag to grow.	☐
Mould can grow on bread.	☐

2

b Explain one way in which the growth of mould can be slowed down.

_____

_____

1

TOTAL

4

2

The teacher of Class 6 shows the children five objects.
They bury the objects in a pot of soil.
They put the pot in the garden.
They will look at the objects again in three weeks' time.

c Tick two objects which will begin to rot away after three weeks.

plastic pen ☐

cabbage leaf ☐

steel teaspoon ☐

apple ☐

thick wooden stick ☐

1

The teacher brought in some fresh grass cuttings in a bag.
He put a thermometer in the bag.
The class noted the readings on the thermometer for five days.

Day	Temperature °C
1	25
2	30
3	35
4	40
5	40

d Use the data to draw a line on this graph.

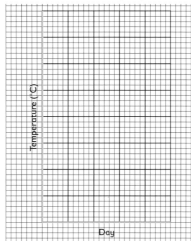

3

e Explain why you think the temperature of the grass cuttings increased.

_____

TOTAL

1

5

3

Human blood circulation

4 Write the name of the part of the blood circulation which is described below.

1

a It pumps blood.

_____

1

b They carry blood away from the heart.

_____

1

c They carry blood back to the heart.

_____

1

d They are the tiny blood vessels that carry blood all over the body.

_____

Look at this diagram

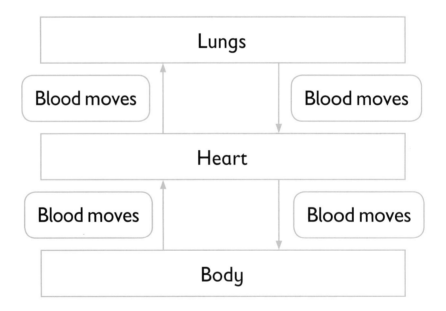

1

Write T(true) or F(false) next to each of these sentences below.

1

e Blood from the heart is pumped to the lungs and the
rest of the body.

TOTAL

f Blood is pumped from the lungs direct to the rest of the body.

6

Health and hygiene

5 a Tom wants to stay healthy.

Write T(true) or F(false) next to each of these ideas.

To stay healthy you need to eat a balanced diet. ☐

1

To stay healthy you must never eat sweets. ☐

You need plenty of sleep to stay healthy. ☐

You need exercise to stay healthy. ☐

You must eat an apple every day to stay healthy. ☐

b Tom's younger sister wants to know why she has to wash her hands before eating her sandwich.
Explain why she needs to wash her hands before eating.
Use the word **bacteria** in your explanation.

1

_____

c Tom's younger sister wants to know why we store meat in the fridge.
Explain why we store meat in the fridge.
Use the word **bacteria** in your explanation.

1

_____

d Tom's younger sister wants to know why we have to brush our teeth.
Explain why we brush our teeth daily.
Use the word **bacteria** in your explanation.

1

_____

TOTAL

4

Weighing boxes

6   Jim and Raj are using spring balances to pull boxes.

Raj uses the spring balance to measure the force needed to move the box. It measures the pull in newtons (N).

a   What force makes it hard to move the box?

_____

1

b   How much force is needed to pull the box?

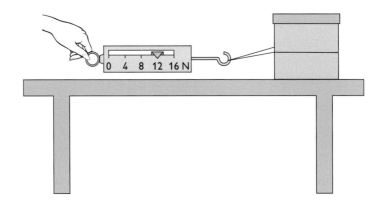

1

_____

c   Raj says it will need less force to pull the box along the smooth table top. Jim says they will need less force on the rough path. Who do you agree with?

_____

1

d   Explain your idea.

_____

1

_____

_____

_____

TOTAL

4

Mirrors

7   **a**   Tick two boxes.
Mirrors reflect light very well because they are:

shiny	☐
translucent	☐
solid	☐
hard	☐
opaque	☐
strong	☐
transparent	☐
smooth	☐

2

   b   Kate is looking at the flowers in the mirror.
Draw arrows to show how she sees the flowers.

2

TOTAL

4

The solar system

8 This is a diagram of the Sun, Moon and Earth.

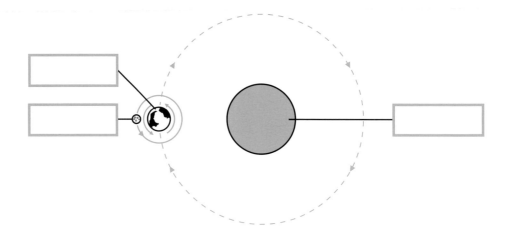

a Write labels on the diagram to show the Earth, Sun and Moon.

1

b What shape is the Sun?

_____

1

c Describe TWO ways in which the Earth moves.

_____

_____

2

d Circle how long it takes for the Earth to orbit the Sun.

1

a day   a month

a year   a millennium

Gravity

9 a Tick the correct sentence.

   Gravity is a force that pulls us down. ☐

   Gravity is a force that pushes us down. ☐

   1

   b Kalid drew a diagram of the Earth.
      He drew four children standing on the Earth.
      On his diagram below, draw in the force of gravity on each of the
      children.

   1

   c Look again at the diagram above.
      Imagine that each child is holding a piece of string with a weight on the
      end.
      Draw in all four of these strings with weights. Show how they would
      hang.

   1

   TOTAL

   3

Identifying animals

1

Write the names of these two animals.
Use the key below to help you.

 a _____   b _____

has it got 4 legs?

yes → no →

has it got a furry body?   does it have feathers?

yes → no →   yes → no →

has it got
big ears?   has it got
a shell?   swallow   does it have
a scaly body?

yes → no →   yes → no →   yes → no →

| hare | platypus | terrapin | gecko | cobra | tarantula |

c According to this key, which animal has a scaly body?

_____

1

1

1

TOTAL

3

Woodlice

2   Jack is experimenting with woodlice.
He wants to find out the sort of place they like to live.
He makes one end of a box dry and bright.
He makes the other end damp and dark.

He puts five woodlice in the box.

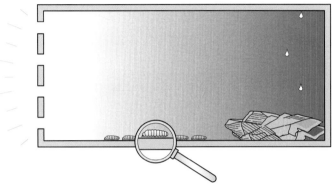

a   What factor is Jack changing in this experiment?
Tick one box.

the woodlice ☐

the places they might live ☐

the number of woodlice ☐

1

b   What factor is he keeping the same?
Tick one box.

the woodlice ☐

the places they might live ☐

1

c   What can he measure at the end of the experiment?
Tick one box.

the woodlice ☐

the places they might live ☐

the number of woodlice ☐

1

1

d   Alice says woodlice are insects.
Is she right?

Tick one box.

yes ☐

no ☐

1

TOTAL

e   Explain your answer to question **d**.

_____

5

Testing a car launcher

3   Some children tested a car launcher, an elastic band that flicked cars along a
    smooth floor.

They stretched the elastic by different amounts.

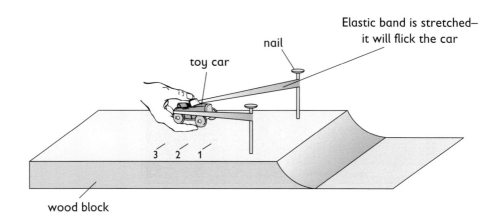

They recorded their results on a table.

	Distance travelled (cm)		
	Test 1	**Test 2**	**Test 3**
Pulled back 1 cm	45	50	40
Pulled back 2 cm	55	60	20
Pulled back 3 cm	66	60	63

a   What pattern do you notice?

_____

_____

_____

b   Why did the children do each test three times?

_____

_____

_____

c   One of the results does not fit the pattern.
    Circle this result on the table.

1

1

1

TOTAL

3

12

Cooking

4   Kim and her dad were working in the kitchen.

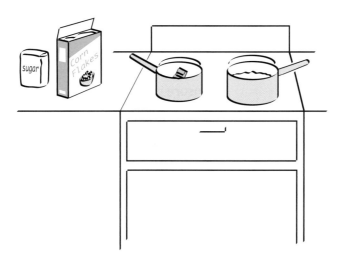

a   Kim added some sugar to her coffee.
Circle what happened to the sugar.

It mixed in.   It dissolved.   It disappeared.   1

b   She heated some butter in a frying pan.
Circle what happened to the butter.

It melted.   It became solid.   It mixed in.   1

c   Her dad fried an egg.
Circle what happened to the egg.

It became solid.   It stayed liquid.   It evaporated.   1

d   Write *yes* or write *no* in the four shaded boxes.

	Does it dissolve in water?	**Does it melt in a warm pan?**
Salt		
Chocolate		

4

TOTAL

7

Scientific units

5   **a**   Connect each unit or measurement to its definition.

ml	measure of heat
sec	measure of small mass
cm	measure of short distance
°C	measure of force
g	measure of large mass
N	measure of volume
kg	measure of short period of time

b   Connect each unit to the instrument which is usually used to measure it. One of the instruments can be used to measure more than one unit.

s	thermometer
cm	ruler
°C	beam balance
g	spring balance
N	stopwatch
kg	

Speed

To work out how fast something is travelling you multiply the distance travelled per second.

A bike which travelled 3 metres in one second is travelling at 3 metres per second.

c   How far would the bike travel in two seconds?

_____

d   How long would it take to travel 12 metres?

_____

7

6

1

1

TOTAL

15

Magnets

6   Look at these pairs of magnets.

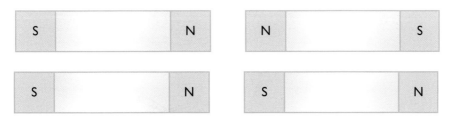

a   Draw arrows to show the force in each of the pictures.

b   Children wanted to test the strength of some magnets.
    They put a steel paper clip next to a ruler and measure how
    far away each magnet will attract the clip.

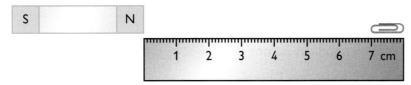

Here are their results.

	Distance from which it attracts the clip (mm)
Horseshoe magnet	12
Small bar magnet	7
Large bar magnet	9

Which is the strongest magnet?

_____

c   Which of these materials are attracted to magnets?
    Tick two.

steel   ☐

brass   ☐

copper   ☐

iron   ☐

diamond   ☐

plastic   ☐

tin   ☐

aluminium   ☐

2

1

2

TOTAL

5

Heating water

7 Water in this pan is being heated.
The wooden handle does not get as hot as the pan.

a Explain why the wooden handle is not as hot as the metal pan.

_____

_____

1

b After a few minutes boiling there is less water in the pan.
Explain why there is less water in the pan after a few minutes boiling.

_____

_____

1

c Complete each sentence below

You use a _____ to measure temperature.

The _____ of the boiling water is 100°C.

2

d Tick the name of the units we use to measure temperature.

Grams ☐

Celsius ☐

Volume ☐

Millimetres ☐

1

TOTAL

5

The water cycle

8   This drawing shows the water cycle.

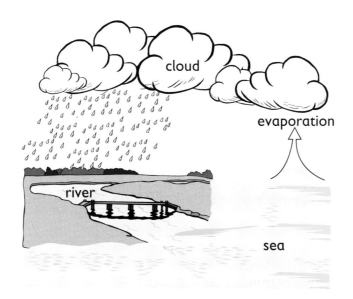

a   Put these parts of the water cycle in the correct order.
The first one has been done.

Rain falls from clouds.   ☐

Clouds are formed by condensation.   ☐

Water flows back to the sea in rivers.   ☐

Water evaporates from the sea.   1

                                           1

b   Tick one box to say what clouds are made from:

water vapour   ☐

tiny water drops   ☐

air and water vapour mixed together   ☐

                                           1

c   Water evaporates off the sea.
Why is rain not salty?

_____

_____

                                           1

TOTAL

3

Living things

1

Pam and Ali wanted to find out about caterpillars.
They looked in a garden.
They counted the caterpillars they found.

On the soil   0

On cabbages   12

On the grass   0

On nettles   3

a   Write T(true) or F(false) next to each sentence.

All the caterpillars were on the cabbages.

There were no caterpillars on the soil or grass.

Most caterpillars in this garden eat cabbage.

b   Pam and Ali noticed that the caterpillars on cabbages were green.
They were difficult to see on the green cabbage leaves.
Explain why caterpillars are often the same colour as the background they live on.

_____

c   Why do some gardeners not like caterpillars?

_____

3

1

1

TOTAL

5

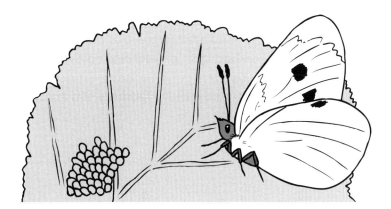

d The caterpillar is one stage in the life cycle of the cabbage white butterfly.
Number the stages in the life cycle.
The first one has been done for you.

The eggs hatch into caterpillars.

Female cabbage white butterflies lay eggs on cabbages.

The caterpillars eat leaves and grow larger.

A butterfly emerges from the pupa.

Adult butterflies mate. | 1 |

The caterpillar forms a pupa.

5

e Caterpillars are eaten by birds such as blue tits. These are eaten in turn
by cats. Write a food chain for cats, blue tits, caterpillars and cabbages.

 _____ ➔ _____ ➔ _____ ➔ _____

4

f To which family group do the animals in the food chain belong?
Draw two lines to connect them to the correct group.
The arrows for the blue tit have been done for you.

caterpillar	mammal
blue tit	invertebrate
cat	vertebrate
	insect
	bird

2

TOTAL

11

19

Animals with a backbone

2   Humans have backbones. They are members of the group called mammals. Write the name of each animal group described below.

     a   This group of animals are covered in feathers and hatch from hard shelled eggs.

_____

     b   This group of animals live in water. They breathe using gills. They lay eggs in water.

_____

     c   This group of animals are covered in damp skin. They lay their eggs in water but most spend their lives on land.

_____

     d   Most of this group of animals live on land. They breathe using lungs. They lay eggs which have a leathery case.

_____

     e   This group of animals are covered in hair. Their young are born alive and are fed on milk.

_____

Underline the odd one out in each group below.

     f   frog   toad   turtle

     g   crocodile   salmon   shark

     h   bear   tiger   cobra

     i   whale   dog   shark

1
1
1
1
1
1
1
1

TOTAL

9

Sounds

3   Anna has a guitar.
She plucks a string to make a low pitched sound.
She plucks a string to make a high pitched sound.

Anna asks Joe to tell her which sound he can hear.
She asks him to move away until he cannot hear one of the sounds.

a   What does Anna want to find out?
Tick one box.

Whether the pitch of the string make a different sound. ☐

The furthest distance that you can hear different pitched sounds. ☐

How far away Joe gets. ☐

1

b   To make it a fair test what TWO things does she keep the same each time?

the person who is listening ☐

the guitar ☐

the distance ☐

2

c   She measures the distance at which Joe can still hear each sound.
Which units will she use? Circle one.

kilograms   degrees   metres   cubic centimetres

1

d   Why do Joe and Anna need to do this test in a quiet place?

They do the test in a quiet place so that _____

_____ .

1

TOTAL

5

21

Circuits

4 Tariq has made three circuits.

a Tick the box to show the circuit in which the bulbs are brightest.
Put a cross in the box of the circuit where the bulbs are dimmest.

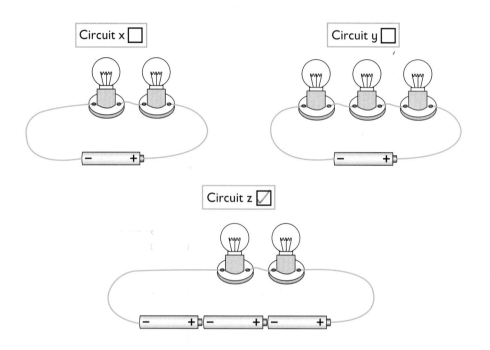

Circuit x ☐

Circuit y ☐

Circuit z ☑

b Explain why the circuit you crossed has the dimmest bulbs.

 Y because it has three bulbs and one battery.

c Draw the circuit diagram for circuit y.

1

1

1

1

TOTAL

4

5 Here are three drawings of circuits.

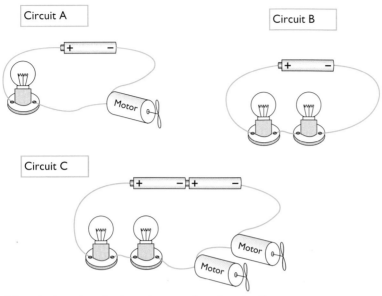

a Match the circuit drawing to the circuit diagram.
Write the matching letter in the box next to the circuit diagram.

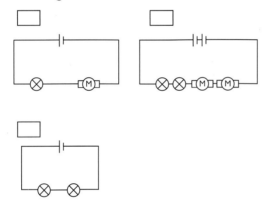

b Draw a circuit diagram showing a motor, an open switch and a cell.

c Will the motor work in this circuit?

_____

d Explain your answer.

_____

Shadows

6 Jim makes a shadow puppet.
He moves it nearer and further away from the projector.

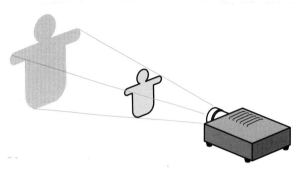

Kate measures the height of the shadow.
She draws a graph of her results.

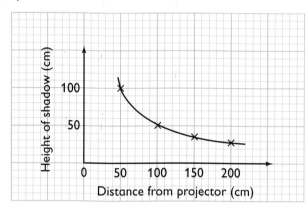

a What was the height of the shadow when the puppet was 100 cm from the projector?

_____

1

b In what way did the shadow change as the puppet moved away from the projector?

_____

1

c Tick the best explanation for how the shadow was formed.

The shadow was formed when the puppet blocked the light of the projector. ☐

The shadow was formed when the reflection of the puppet was on the screen. ☐

The shadow was formed when the puppet made a shape on the screen. ☐

1

TOTAL

3

7   **a**   Tina is looking at her birthday candles.
Add an arrow to show how she sees the light from the candles.

1

b   Saida is reading her map under the street lamp.
Add arrows to show how she sees the map.

1

1

c   Saida, John and Tina are talking about how we see the Moon.
Tick the best explanation.

We see the Moon because it is a source of light. ☐

We see the Moon because it reflects sunlight to us. ☐

The Sun's light passes through the Moon and it
reaches us in that way. ☐

TOTAL

3

The human body

1 This graph shows Kim's weight as she grows older.

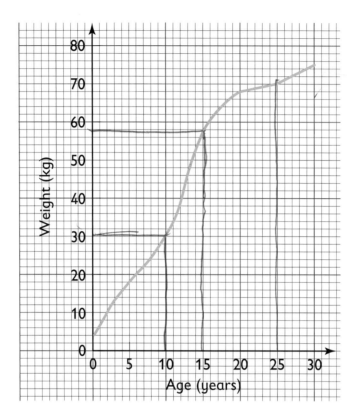

a How heavy was Kim on her 10th birthday?

_____30_____ kg

b Write T(true) or F(false) next to each statement below.

Kim weighed 57kg on her 15th birthday. | T |

Kim grew heavier each year until she was 25 years old. | F |

Kim stopped growing heavier after she was 10. | F |

Kim stopped growing heavier after she was 20. | F |

1

4

TOTAL

5

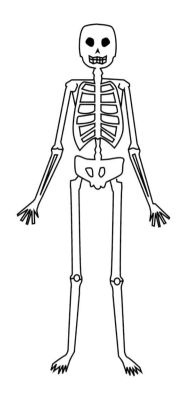

2 **a** Join the description to the name of the bones or joint.

A hinge joint in your leg   Hip

A ball and socket joint at the top of your leg   Ribs

The bones which protect your lungs   Knee

The bones which protect the brain   Ankle

The joint which allows your foot to move   Skull

5

b Tick the correct sentence.

Each of our four fingers has three joints.   ☑

Our thumbs have four joints.   ☒

Each of our four fingers has one joint.   ☒

1

TOTAL

Invertebrates

3 This very large group of animals do not have a backbone.
Write the name of each animal group described below.

a This group of animals have six legs and their bodies are divided into three parts.

b This group of animals have eight legs and many of them spin webs. Scorpions are in this group.

c This group of animals have soft, long and thin bodies like tubes.

d Most of this group live in the sea. They include crabs and lobsters. Woodlice are in this group. They live on land.

e This group of animals cover their body in slime. They have soft bodies and at the front they have feelers and eyes on stalks.

Underline the odd one out in each group below.

f bee   wasp   spider

g earthworm   dragonfly   beetle

h woodlouse   spider   crab

i scorpion   grasshopper   tarantula

1

1

1

1

1

1

1

1

TOTAL

9

Materials

4

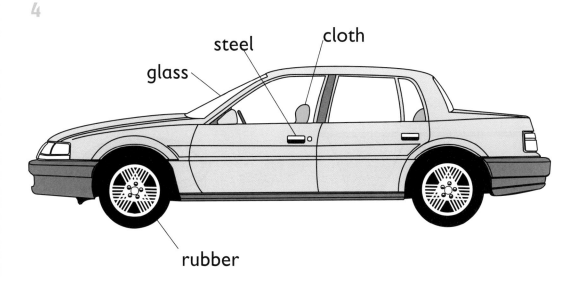

glass   steel   cloth

rubber

a   Give one reason why glass is a good material for a car windscreen.

_____

_____

1

b   Give one reason why steel is a good material for making a car door handle.

_____

_____

1

c   Give one reason why rubber is a good material for tyres.

_____

_____

1

d   Give one reason why cloth is a good material for seat covers.

_____

_____

1

TOTAL

4

5 Ryan and Saida are separating mixtures.
Suggest ways they could separate these mixtures.

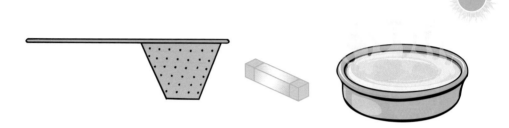

a A mixture of peas and flour.

_____
_____

1

b A mixture of sand and small iron nails.

_____
_____

1

c A mixture of sand and salt.

_____
_____

1

d A solution of water and salt.

_____
_____

1

e Oil and water.

_____
_____

1

TOTAL

5

Testing the strength of paper

6   Nadim and Ella were testing the strength of paper.

They cut strips of paper. They folded over one end and held it with sticky tape.

They used a spring balance to hold the folded end and they pulled the other end until the paper began to tear.

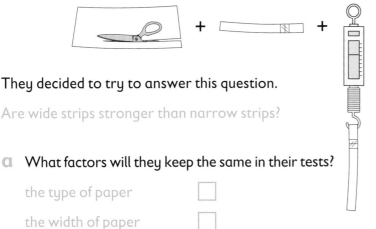

They decided to try to answer this question.

Are wide strips stronger than narrow strips?

a   What factors will they keep the same in their tests?

the type of paper   ☐

the width of paper   ☐

the length of paper strip   ☐

This is the bar chart they made from their results.

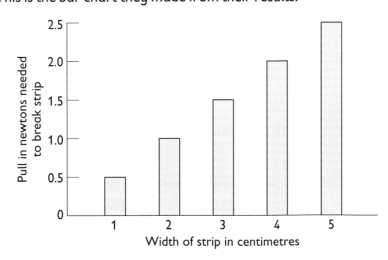

b   Use the bar chart to fill in the empty box in this table.

	1 cm wide	2 cm wide	3 cm wide	4 cm wide	5 cm wide
Pull needed to break	0.5 N	1 N	1.5 N		2.5 N

2

1

TOTAL

3

31

Nadim and Ella decided to compare the strength of different types of paper.

They decided to test:

- tissue paper
- thick wallpaper
- drawing paper.

c Predict their order of strength:

| weakest paper | medium strength paper | strongest paper |

_____ _____ _____

1

d Explain why you have put them in this order.

_____

_____

1

Nadim and Ella decided to test the strength of shiny magazine paper and newspaper.

They tested each paper three times.

They put five drops of water on each paper and tested three times again.

Pull needed to break different paper (newtons)

	Dry newspaper	Wet newspaper	Dry shiny magazine paper	Wet shiny magazine paper
1st try	2	0.5	4	3
2nd try	2	0.2	5	2.5
3rd try	2.5	0.4	3	3

2

e Write TWO things this table tells you about the strength of newspaper and shiny magazine paper.

_____

_____

TOTAL

4

Sound

7 Kim is standing near the table. She listens to Dan as he scratches the table with his fingernail.

a What material is the sound travelling through to reach Kim's ears?

_____

b Kim stays the same distance from Dan.
She presses her ear to the table.
Through what material is the sound travelling to Kim's ear?

_____

c With her ear pressed to the table Kim can hear the sound more clearly.
Explain why this happens.

_____

_____

d Kim puts a woolly jumper between her ear and the table.
Predict what will happen to the loudness of the sound she hears.

_____

_____

e Explain your idea.

_____

_____

TOTAL

5

The Moon, the Earth and the Sun

8   This is a drawing to show the Moon orbiting the Earth.

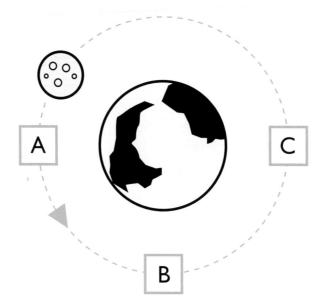

1

a   How long does it take for the Moon to go from A to B?

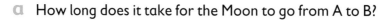

_____

1

b   How long does it take for the Moon to go from A to C?

_____

1

c   The Moon does not give out any light of its own.
Describe how we can see the Moon.

_____

_____

1

d   The Moon appears to be about the same size as the Sun in the sky.
Explain why you think the Sun and Moon appear to be the same size.

_____

_____

TOTAL

4

Living in water

1 The killer whale is adapted to live in water.

a Write two ways in which it is adapted to live in water.

_____

_____

2

b The killer whale is a hunter.
Write two ways in which it is adapted to hunt.

_____

_____

2

c The animals pictured below are all adapted to live in water.

Link each one to the way it is adapted to life in water.

4

has armour that helps to protect it from predators
has eight legs and can grab prey items
has a thick layer of fat that keeps it warm
has a covering of feathers that helps keep it warm in water

TOTAL

8

Adapted to habitats

2   Some animals are camouflaged.
    This means they blend in with their surroundings.

a   Tigers are hunters. They blend in with the jungle.
    Why does this help them?

1

 _____

_____

b   Frogs are eaten by many animals. They blend in with pond weeds.
    Why does this help them?

1

 _____

_____

c   Some animals want to show up clearly.
    Wasps and bees are easy to see with their black and yellow stripes.
    Why do they want to show up so clearly?

1

1

 _____

_____

TOTAL

d   Wildlife film makers do not want to frighten the animals.
    What colour clothes should people wear when filming animals in a sandy
    desert?

4

 _____

Materials

3   a   Match each material to its description.
Draw a line from the description (left) to the material (right).

magnetic metal	air
light and strong – used for buildings	iron
a mixture of gases	wood
transparent material that breaks easily	plastic
light and soft – easily made into shapes	glass

5

   b Light goes through some materials.

Write these words in the correct spaces below.

translucent   transparent   opaque

Clear glass is a _____ material. That means you can see through it.

Materials like tissue paper let some light through. These materials are

_____.

Materials that do not let light pass through are called _____.

3

   c Write T(true) or F(false) next to each statement below.

Wood is opaque. ☐

All glass is totally transparent. ☐

Cardboard is opaque. ☐

4

Thin sheets of paper are usually translucent. ☐

TOTAL ◯

12

Candles

4 Dylan weighs a candle.
He burns it for one hour.
He weighs the candle again.
He does this for four hours.
He draws a bar chart to show the changes in weight.

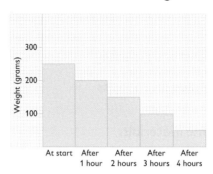

a How much did the candle weigh at the start of the experiment?

1

b How much did the candle weigh after 3 hours?

1

c Explain why the candle's weight changed.

1

d Can you reverse the changes in the candle?

1

e Dylan and his teacher put a jam jar over a small candle.
Predict what will happen to the candle flame.

_____

_____

1

f Explain your idea.

_____

2

TOTAL

7

38

Fossils

5 Fossils show how animals were adapted to protect and feed themselves.
These fossils are from the time of dinosaurs.

a Write how this dinosaur protected itself.

_____

_____

_____

b Write how this dinosaur was able to feed itself.

_____

_____

_____

c Write how this dinosaur was adapted to chase and catch its prey.

_____

_____

_____

d Write how this dinosaur was adapted to warm up quickly in the sun.

_____

_____

_____

All dinosaurs were a kind of reptile.

e Fill in the blank spaces.

All reptiles have _____ skin.

They lay _____ eggs.

All reptiles breathe _____.

f Name two reptiles which are alive today.

_____

1

1

1

1

3

2

TOTAL

9

39

Parachutes

6 Some children tested parachutes. They made all the parachutes from thin sheets of plastic. They had three parachutes of different sizes.

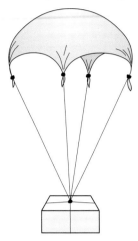 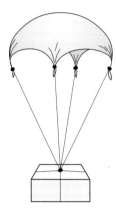 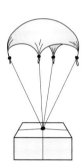

a Which question were they investigating?

Do heavy parachutes fall more slowly than lighter ones? ☐

Do large parachutes fall more slowly than smaller ones? ☐

Do plastic parachutes fall more slowly than paper ones? ☐

This graph shows the results of their test.

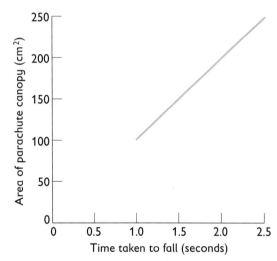

b How long would it take for a parachute of area 150 cm² to fall?

_____

c How long would it take for a parachute of area 300 cm² to fall?

_____

Use the graph to help you.

1

1

1

TOTAL

3

40

Some other children changed the mass on a parachute.

These are their results.

	20 g	40 g	60 g
Time taken to fall	4 seconds	3 seconds	2.5 seconds

d   Draw axes with scales on the graph paper below.

Mark the three results and join up the marks to make a graph.

Time taken to fall (seconds)

Mass of the parachute (g)

5

Kim and Tammy made two parachutes out of different materials.

They used tissue and net curtain.

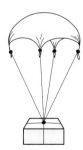   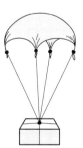

e   Write THREE things they had to keep the same for each parachute.

_____

_____

_____

3

1

TOTAL

They found that the tissue parachute fell slower than the net parachute.

f   Suggest one reason why this happened.

_____

9

Answers

Tests 1–4

The words in brackets are not part of the answer you should expect from children.
All text in brackets is explanatory to help parents/guardians when discussing the answers with their children.

Question number	Answer	Mark
TEST 1		
1	Plants and animals	
a	oak tree, grass, wheat, bee, crocodile are all living things	5
b	pine tree, carrot, seaweed, tulip, nettle, cactus are all plants	6
c	They are making food from sunlight.	1
2	Bread and yeast	
a	Jim is correct. Yeast is alive because it feeds on flour (yeast also feeds on sugar).	1
3	Rotting	
a	The two correct ideas are: Mould grows best in a warm place. Mould can grow on bread. (award mark only if both are correct)	2
b	Ideas will vary but acceptable are: refrigerate / keep cool / freeze / heat and keep in sealed jar or tin / cover in salt / cover in sugar	1
c	The cabbage leaf and apple are likely to have started to rot away. (award mark only if both are correct)	1
d	The temperature could also be shown using a different scale (such as going up in 10s) and the day markings could start on the extreme left.	up to 3 (One mark if both axes are labelled correctly. One mark if the five coordinates are shown correctly by dots or small crosses. One mark if line joins the dots or crosses.)
e	The temperature increased as the micro-organisms / fungus / bacteria / began to break down / digest / change / rot the grass cuttings.	1
4	Human blood circulation	
a	The heart	1
b	Artery	1
c	Veins	1
d	Capillaries	1
e	True	1
f	False	1
5	Health and hygiene	
a	T, F, T, T, F	1 (One mark only if all are correct)
b	Some bacteria on your hands will make you ill if they get onto your food and into your mouth. You need to wash off the bacteria to stop them getting on your food.	1
c	Bacteria will breed very quickly on meat in warm places. They breed much more slowly in cold places.	1
d	Bacteria can live in sugary deposits on dirty teeth. (This deposit is called plaque.) The bacteria then produce acid that attacks tooth enamel.	1
6	Weighing boxes	
a	Friction	1
b	12 newtons (12N)	1
c	Raj	1
d	Smooth surfaces usually have less friction than rough ones. For instance, a smooth slide is more slippy than a rough one.	1
7	Mirrors	
a	shiny and smooth	2
b		2
8	The solar system	
a		1
b	The Sun is a sphere (spherical or like a ball).	1

Question number	Answer	Mark
c	The Earth turns (spins) on its axis. The Earth orbits the Sun.	2
d	The Earth takes **a year** to orbit the Sun.	1
9	Gravity	
a	Gravity is a force that pulls us down.	1
b and c		2
TEST 2		
1	Identifying animals	
a and b	a Tarantula b Terrapin	2
c	Cobra	1
2	Woodlice	
a	The places they might live	1
b	The woodlice	1
c	The number of woodlice	1
d	No, woodlice are not insects.	1
e	Woodlice do not have six legs. All insects have six legs. (Woodlice are crustaceans. These, like insects, have an external skeleton and jointed limbs. Crustaceans have a different number of limbs and a different body pattern.)	1
3	Testing a car launcher	
a	The more the band is pulled back the greater the distance travelled by the car.	1
b	They did it three times to get an average / to make sure they would notice any flukes or errors.	1
c	Table should have 20 circled.	1
4	Cooking	
a	It dissolved.	1
b	It melted.	1
c	It became solid.	1
d	Salt – dissolves in water but does not melt in a warm pan. Chocolate – does not dissolve in water but melts in a warm pan.	4
5	Scientific units	
a	ml is a measure of volume sec is a measure of time cm is a measure of distance °C is a measure of heat g is a measure of small mass N is a measure of force kg is a measure of large mass	7
b	s is measured by a stopwatch cm is measured by a ruler °C is measured by a thermometer g is measured by a beam balance N is measured by a spring balance kg is measured by a beam balance	6
c	6 metres	1
d	4 seconds	1
6	Magnets	
a		1
		1
b	The horseshoe magnet is strongest.	1
c	steel and iron	2
7	Heating water	
a	Wood is not a good conductor of heat / wood conducts heat less well than metal / metal is a better conductor of heat than wood.	1
b	Some of the water has evaporated / boiled away.	1
c	thermometer temperature	2
d	Celsius	1
8	The water cycle	
a	Rain falls from clouds. 3 Clouds are formed by condensation. 2 Water flows back to the sea in rivers. 4 Water evaporates from the sea. 1 (all have to be in correct order for one mark)	1
b	tiny water drops (the water vapour condenses to form clouds)	1
c	When water evaporates it leaves behind any dissolved solids.	1

Answers

Question number	Answer	Mark
TEST 3		
1	*Living things*	
a	F T T	3
b	The caterpillars were camouflaged / blended into the background to avoid being eaten.	1
c	Some gardeners do not like caterpillars because they eat the plants they grow.	1
d	The eggs hatch into caterpillars. 3 Female cabbage white butterflies lay eggs on cabbages. 2 The caterpillars eat leaves and grow larger. 4 A butterfly emerges from the pupa. 6 Adult butterflies mate. 1 The caterpillar forms a pupa. 5	5
e	cabbage ➡ caterpillar ➡ blue tit ➡ cat	4
f	caterpillar, blue tit, cat → mammal, invertebrate, vertebrate, insect, bird	2
2	*Animals with a backbone*	
a	birds	1
b	fish	1
c	amphibians	1
d	reptiles	1
e	mammals	1
f	turtle	1
g	crocodile	1
h	cobra	1
i	shark	1
3	*Sounds*	
a	The furthest distance that you can hear different pitched sounds.	1
b	She keeps the person and the guitar the same.	2
c	metres	1
d	So they are not distracted.	1
4	*Circuits*	
a	circuit z should be ticked circuit y should be crossed	1 1
b	Answers will vary – these are acceptable: The electricity is shared between three bulbs. There is only one cell and three bulbs. The resistance of the three bulbs is greater than that of the two bulbs in the other circuits.	1
c		1
5a		3
b		3
c	No.	1
d	The motor will not work, as the switch is open / the circuit is not complete. Also accept a response that the motor will only work if the switch is closed.	1
6	*Shadows*	
a	50 cm	1
b	It got smaller.	1
c	The shadow was formed when the puppet blocked the light of the projector.	1
7a		1
b		1
c	We see the Moon because it reflects sunlight to us.	1

Question number		Answer	Mark
TEST 4			
1		The human body	
	a	30 kg	1
	b	T T F F	4
2a		A hinge joint in your leg knee A ball and socket joint at the top of your leg hip The bones which protect your lungs ribs The bones which protect the brain skull The joint which allows your foot to move ankle	5
	b	Each of our four fingers has three joints.	1
3		Invertebrates	
	a	Insects	1
	b	Spiders	1
	c	Worms	1
	d	Crustaceans	1
	e	Mollusc	1
	f	Spider	1
	g	Earthworm	1
	h	Spider	1
	i	Grasshopper	1
4		Materials	
	a	It is transparent (accept see-through).	1
	b	It is strong.	1
	c	It is flexible (accept bendy / squashy), or it has good grip.	1
	d	It feels nice / easy to clean / not sweaty / soft (accept any answer which implies comfort).	1
5a		They should use a sieve. (The peas will stay in the sieve and the flour will fall through.)	1
	b	Use a magnet to attract the nails. The sand will not be attracted. (Some children will correctly say that the magnet should be wrapped in paper, or a bag, so it is easy to remove the nails.)	1
	c	Add water to dissolve the salt. The sand will not dissolve.	1
	d	Let the water evaporate. The salt will be left behind. (Very able children might additionally answer that the water can be condensed on a cold surface.)	1
	e	The oil will float on top of the water and can be poured or spooned off the top.	1
6		Testing the strength of paper	
	a	They will keep these two factors the same: the type of paper and the length of paper strip.	2
	b	2.0 N	1
	c	The best prediction is that weakest = tissue paper, medium = drawing paper, strongest = thick wallpaper.	1
	d	Thicker paper is usually stronger than thin paper.	1
	e	Two from the following: Shiny paper is stronger than newspaper. Newspaper is weaker than shiny paper. Newspaper becomes very weak when wet. Shiny paper is weaker when wet. Shiny paper is not as affected by water as newspaper is.	2
7		Sound	
	a	Sound is travelling through table and air.	1
	b	The table. (Some children may also correctly add: "through the air in her ear canal!")	1
	c	Sound travels better through solids than it does through the air. (Also allow sound travels better through the wood / table than through the air.)	1
	d	The sound will get muffled / not heard at all.	1
	e	The sound will not travel well through soft materials / The jumper acts like an ear protector.	1
8		The Moon, the Earth and the Sun	
	a	It takes one week for the Moon to go from A to B (quarter orbit).	1
	b	It takes two weeks for the Moon to go from A to C.	1
	c	The Moon reflects the Sun's light.	1
	d	The Moon is much smaller but much closer to us than the Sun.	1

National Curriculum Levels

Test 1	47 marks
Test 2	46 marks
Test 3	48 marks
Test 4	45 marks

	Level 2	Level 3	Level 4	Level 5
Test 1	Below 14	14–23	24–36	37–47
Test 2	Below 11	11–26	27–33	34–46
Test 3	Below 14	14–26	27–35	36–48
Test 4	Below 10	10–20	21–34	35–45

Test 5

Question number	Answer	Mark
1	Living in water	
a	Two from: It is streamline. It has fins. It has good senses underwater. It can swim quickly.	2
b	Two from: It can swim very quickly. It has sharp teeth. it has good sense of hearing underwater.	2
c	A duck has a covering of feathers that helps keep it warm in water. A seal has a thick layer of fat that keeps it warm. An octopus has eight legs and can grab prey items. A lobster has armour that helps to protect it from predators.	4
2	Adapted to habitats	
a	They cannot be seen by their prey. (Accept also human hunters cannot see them easily.)	1
b	They cannot be seen easily by predators.	1
c	They want to warn animals to keep away.	1
d	They should wear sandy coloured clothes (to blend in with the surroundings and not scare the animals).	1
3	Materials	
a	Magnetic metal → iron Transparent material that breaks easily → glass Light and strong – used for buildings → wood Light and soft – easily made into shapes → plastic A mixture of gases → air	5
b	Clear glass is a **transparent** material. That means you can see through it. Materials like tissue paper let some light through. These materials are **translucent**. Materials that do not let light pass through are called **opaque**.	3
c	Wood is opaque. T Cardboard is opaque. T All glass is totally transparent. F Thin sheets of paper are usually translucent. T	4
4	Candles	
a	250 grams	1
b	100 grams	1
c	The candle wax was burnt / the wax evaporated in the flame / the wax was changed into a gas.	1
d	No you cannot reverse this change.	1
e	The candle flame will go out after a short while.	1
f	The flame will go out because there is no oxygen / air reaching the flame.	2
5	Fossils	
a	It had horns and a bony head.	1
b	It reached up into the trees with a long neck.	1
c	It had strong front legs and grasping claws.	1
d	It had plates on its back which captured the heat of the sun.	1
e	All reptiles have scaly skin. They lay leathery eggs. All reptiles breathe air.	3
f	For example crocodile, tortoise, snake, lizard, etc.	2
6	Parachutes	
a	They were investigating "Do large parachutes fall more slowly than smaller ones?".	1
b	It would take **1.5 seconds** (accept $1\frac{1}{2}$) for a 150 cm² parachute to fall.	1
c	It would take **3 seconds** for a 300 cm² parachute to fall.	1
d		5 *(2 marks for axis scales, 2 marks for plotted points, 1 mark for smooth curve)*
e	Three from the following: • same mass on parachute • same lengths of strings to hold the mass • similar way of timing • same size of canopy • same distance dropped • same way each was dropped	3
f	The net curtain has holes in it so does not trap the air *or* it has less air resistance.	1

National Curriculum Levels

For Test 5 (worth a total of 52 marks), the marks indicate the following levels.

Mark	Below 12	12–22	23–39	40–52
Level	Level 2	Level 3	Level 4	Level 5